Science In Your Life:

LIGHT

LOOK OUT!

Wendy Sadler

www.raintreepublishers.co.uk
Visit our website to find out more information about **Raintree** books.

To order:
☎ Phone 44 (0) 1865 888112
▤ Send a fax to 44 (0) 1865 314091
▢ Visit the Raintree bookshop at **www.raintreepublishers.co.uk** to browse
our catalogue and order online.

First published in Great Britain by Raintree,
Halley Court, Jordan Hill, Oxford OX2 8EJ,
part of Harcourt Education.
Raintree is a registered trademark
of Harcourt Education Ltd.

Editorial: Melanie Copland, Kate Buckingham,
and Lucy Beevor
Design: Victoria Bevan
and Bridge Creative Services Ltd
Picture Research: Hannah Taylor
and Catherine Bevan
Production: Duncan Gilbert

Originated by Chroma Graphics (Overseas) Pte. Ltd
Printed and bound in China by
South China Printing Company

ISBN 1 844 43660 8
10 09 08 07 06
10 9 8 7 6 5 4 3 2 1

**British Library Cataloguing in
Publication Data**
Sadler, Wendy
Light. – (Science in your life)
535
A full catalogue record for this book is available
from the British Library.

Acknowledgements
Alamy Images pp. 16 (BananaStock), 11
(Brand X Pictures), 14 (GOODSHOOT), 17
(Momentum Creative Group), 19 (Nick Hanna),
21 (The National Trust Photolibrary); Corbis pp. 25
(LWA-Sharle Kennedy), 12 (Koopman); Corbis
Royalty Free pp. 15, 22, 26; Getty Images pp. 5, 6,
20, 23 (PhotoDisc); Harcourt Education Ltd pp. 8, 9,
27 (Tudor Photography); Photographers Direct pp. 4
(Antoinette Burton), 24 (Life File Photos Ltd),
10 (Lightphotographic); Photolibrary.com/ Ips co Ltd
p.13; Science Photo Library p. 18 (Tony McConnell);
SeaPics.com p. 7 (Mick McMurray).

Cover photograph of fireworks reproduced with
permission of Getty/BrandX.

Contents

Any words appearing in the text in bold, **like this**, are explained in the glossary.

Light really is all around you! Light helps you to find your way around – indoors and out. It helps you see shapes and colours when you are playing games. The numbers on a clock can light up to tell you the time when it is dark. The morning daylight tells you it is soon time to get up.

When the Sun comes up, it is nearly time to wake up.

Light in your life!

Look at this list of things you might have done today that used light.

- switched on the bathroom light
- read a comic or a book
- looked at the time
- looked in the mirror and seen your face.

Which of these have you done? Can you think of any more things you have done that used light?

Could you catch a ball in the dark?

Where does light come from?

Most light that we use comes from things that are very, very hot. When you are outside in the daytime you can see things because of the light coming from the Sun. The Sun is very hot and this is why it gives out a lot of light. At night-time when we do not have the light from the Sun, it gets dark.

When something gets very hot it starts to glow. This glow gives off light. First of all it glows a red colour, then it gets whiter as it gets hotter.

The wire in a light bulb is called a **filament**. When it gets hot it glows very brightly.

Some things give out light without getting hot. The light and colours on your television screen come from special **chemicals** that glow when **electricity** is fired at them.

Other lights, such as the ones in clock radios, are called **LEDs**. LEDs also use electricity to make light and they do not have to get hot.

Some jelly-fish in the deep, dark parts of the sea can make their own light by mixing special chemicals in their body.

How does light travel?

Light usually travels in straight lines called rays of light. Shadows show how light travels in straight lines. Light can be blocked by objects that you cannot see through. If you put an object between a light and a wall you can make a shadow on the wall.

You can use your hands to make shadow shapes on the wall because light cannot go through your hands.

Light travels very, very quickly. A ray of light could travel around the world in less than 1 second! When you switch a light on you cannot see it move from the light bulb to your eyes because it happens much too quickly.

Light can get bent if it travels from one type of **material** into another. Air is a gas and water is a liquid. If light travels through water and then air, the ray of light gets bent.

Light in your life!

Put a spoon into a glass of water. The spoon looks bent, but it is the light that is bending as it goes from the water to the air.

Light the messenger

Light can be used to send messages because it can travel so quickly. Traffic lights use coloured lights to send a message. Red lights tell you to stop and green lights tell you when to go.

These traffic lights help keep the traffic moving safely and smoothly by using light to send messages.

Light can be made to go around corners using something called an **optical fibre**. This special **material** is as thin as one of the hairs on your head! The light travels along the optical fibre and can carry messages with it.

Light travels to the ends of optical fibres to make this lamp sparkle.

Light in your life!

Get a torch and use it to send a message to a friend without using your voice or a pen and paper! Use Morse code, which is a code that uses just long and short flashes, to send a message. A dot (.) is a short flash and a dash (−) is a long flash. Each letter of the alphabet has its own code. Try sending this message:

. . . − − − . . .

This message means S.O.S (save our souls) and it can be used to call for help. You can find the full Morse code on page 28. Can you send your own message?

Reflection

When light hits an object some of the light will usually bounce off. When light bounces off something it is called a **reflection**. Hard and shiny objects are very good at reflecting light.

A mirror is made of glass and metal. The metal is very shiny so it reflects light well. Without a mirror you could not check your hair in the morning!

The tiny mirrors on this ball reflect light in many directions.

Most objects that we see every day do not give off any light of their own. We see these objects because the light that comes from the Sun or a light bulb reflects off them. The light bouncing off the objects travels into our eyes. When the light reaches our eyes we can see the objects.

The knives and forks on this table are made of shiny metal and reflect a lot of light.

Mirror, mirror on the wall

A mirror is a very **reflective** object that helps you to see what you look like. Light bounces off your face and hits the mirror. The light is then bounced back off the mirror and into your eyes so you can see your own face.

A dentist uses a small mirror to look at your teeth. By holding the mirror at an angle, the dentist can get the light from the back of your mouth to bounce up into his or her eyes.

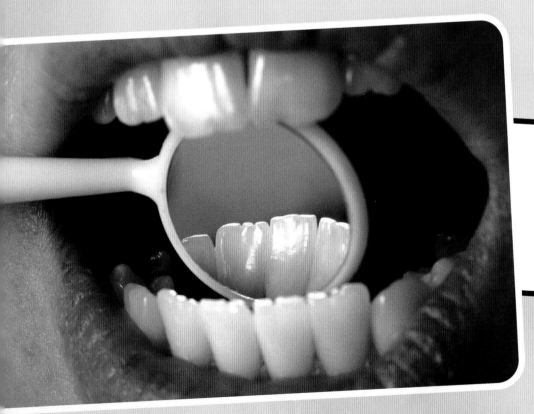

This mirror helps the dentist to see the back of the teeth.

The mountains are reflected in the still waters of the lake, so you can see them twice.

Water can make good reflections, too. If you look at a puddle or a lake you can sometimes see a reflection of the sky. The smooth **surface** of the water is a bit like a mirror. If it is windy and the water has ripples then the light will not reflect so well off the surface.

How do we see?

Our eyes take in light from things around us. Some things, such as light bulbs and television screens, give off their own light. Most things we see do not make their own light. Instead, they **reflect** light that comes from other places.

At the back of your eye there are some special **cells** that **react** to light. These cells build up a pattern of the colours you are seeing. The pattern made at the back of the eye is sent to your brain. Your brain works out what the pattern is. Without our brains our eyes would not be able to see anything!

There are **muscles** in your eyes that can move your eyes around to point at the things you want to look at. The pupils are the black parts of your eyes. Light enters your eyes through the pupils.

When you are in a dark room your pupil gets very large to let in as much light as possible. In a bright place, the pupil gets much smaller.

Light in your life!

Ask a friend to try to move their eyes smoothly from left to right. Look at their eyes while they do it. Do their eyes move smoothly? Now move your finger from left to right and ask them to follow it with their eyes. Now do their eyes move smoothly?

Invisible light

There are some types of light that our eyes cannot see. When you turn the television on with a remote control you are using a type of light called **infrared**. Heat from the Sun, and from our bodies, can also make infrared light.

This picture was taken using a special camera that can pick up infrared light, and turn it into a picture.

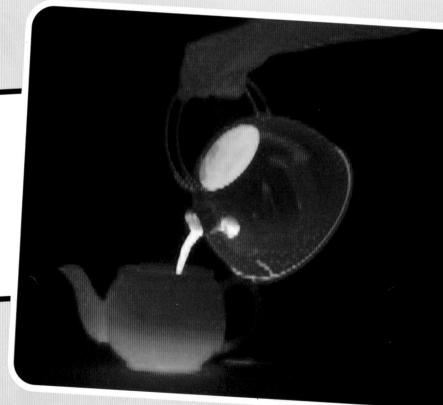

Firefighters can use special cameras that pick up the invisible light and turn it into a picture. This means that they can find people in the dark, or if they are trapped under ground.

Another type of invisible light is called **ultraviolet**. This light comes from the Sun and it can give you sunburn. Sun cream is used to block the ultraviolet (UV) light so that it does not reach your skin.

You should put sun cream on any bits of skin that are not covered up by clothes to protect yourself against ultraviolet light.

What is colour?

White light is a mixture of all the colours in a **rainbow**. You can use a triangle shaped piece of glass to split the light up into all the separate colours. The glass shape is called a **prism**.

Rainbows appear when rain and sunshine happen at the same time. The light from the Sun goes through the raindrops and splits up into all the colours, like passing through a prism. When these colours come into your eye, you see the rainbow.

The colours in the light bend as they travel through the glass. Blue bends more than red, so the colours all split up.

Some windows have lots of different colours in them. They are called stained glass windows.

When an object looks red, this is because it takes in all the other colours in white light except red. We say that it **absorbs** the other colours. The red is **reflected** into our eyes so we see red.

If light is shining through a window you can make colours by using coloured glass. Blue glass will block all the other colours except blue. This means you see blue light shining through that part of the window.

Chemical colours

Some **chemicals** give out coloured light when they get very hot. Street lights sometimes shine with a yellow-orange light because of a chemical called sodium. When sodium gets hot it glows a yellow-orange colour.

Fireworks come in lots of different colours. They are made by mixing different chemicals together. When the fireworks burn they give out coloured light. Fireworks are very dangerous and you should never play with them.

Different chemicals in the fireworks give us displays of different coloured lights.

A telescope collects more light from objects in the sky, so you can see them more clearly.

Astronomers are scientists who look up at the sky to find out more about space, stars, and the planets. They can look at the colours of the stars in the sky and work out what chemicals they are made of. Astronomers use special telescopes to help them see the stars.

Energy from light

Light has **energy**. We can use the energy from light to heat things up. Dark coloured objects are very good at **absorbing** the heat from light. Light coloured objects do not absorb so much heat.

If you put water into a dark coloured container on a sunny day, it can get hot. This is called solar heating. Solar is a word that means: "to do with the Sun".

Solar panels can turn energy from the Sun into electricity. You can sometimes see these on the roofs of houses.

Green plants take in light from the Sun and turn it into energy to make them grow. People and animals eat the plants to get energy. This means that we all get our energy from the Sun. We are all solar powered!

We get our energy by eating food. The energy in the food has come from the Sun because the sunlight helps the plants grow.

What is a laser?

A laser is a special type of light that shines with just one colour. A laser has a thin beam of light that can be very powerful.

The laser beam at a supermarket checkout reads the pattern of lines printed on the packet or tin of food. This pattern is called a barcode. The pattern gives the price and also sends a message to tell the shop what you have bought.

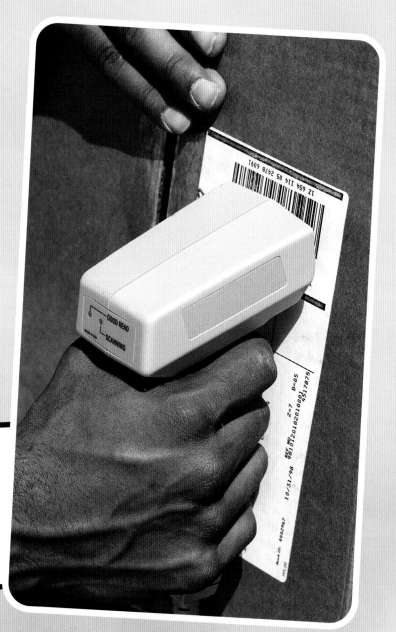

A laser reads the barcode and enters the price you have to pay.

Light is used all around you in many ways. Without it we would not be able to see ourselves in a mirror, play music on our CD player, or see the colours of the world around us. Use your eyes to see if you can find other ways that we use light every day.

Inside a CD player a laser beam reads a pattern of tiny holes on the surface of the disc. The pattern of holes is turned into music!

Facts about light

Try sending your own messages using Morse **code**. All you need is a torch. Remember that a dot (.) is a short flash and a dash (–) is a long flash.

A	.–	S	...
B	–...	T	–
C	–.–.	U	..–
D	–..	V	...–
E	.	W	.– –
F	..–.	X	–..–
G	– –.	Y	–.– –
H	....	Z	– –..
I	..	0	– – – – –
J	.– – –	1	.– – – –
K	–.–	2	..– – –
L	.–..	3	...– –
M	– –	4	....–
N	–.	5	.....
O	– – –	6	–....
P	.– –.	7	– –...
Q	– –.–	8	– – –..
R	.–.	9	– – – –.

Thomas Edison invented the light bulb in 1879, more than 100 years ago!

A light year is a way of measuring really big distances. A light year is the distance that light would travel in 1 year. A light year is 10 trillion kilometres (6 trillion miles!)

Light takes about 8 seconds to get to us from the Sun.

X-rays are a type of light. X-rays can go through your body, but not through your bones. Doctors can use them to see inside you and check for broken bones.

Energy efficient light bulbs use a quarter of the energy of ordinary light bulbs — and they last up to twenty times longer!

Find out more

You can find out more about science in everyday life by talking to your teacher or parents. Your local library will also have books that can help. You will find the answers to many of your questions in this book. If you want to know more, you can use other books and the Internet.

Books to read

Discovering Science: Light and Dark, Rebecca Hunter (Raintree, 2003)

Science Answers: Light, Chris Cooper (Heinemann Library, 2003)

Science Files: Light, Steve Parker (Heinemann Library, 2004)

Using the Internet

Explore the Internet to find out more about light. Try using a search engine such as www.yahooligans.com or www.internet4kids.com, and type in keywords such as "**LED**", "**optical fibre**", and "**prism**".

Glossary

absorb take in. Light can be absorbed by objects.

astronomer someone who studies space, the stars, and planets

cells very tiny pieces that all living things are made from. Different cells in the body do different jobs.

chemical special substance. Everything around us is made of chemicals. Some are natural and some are man-made.

code way of sending messages using numbers, letters, or shapes

electricity form of energy that can be used to make things work. Computers and televisions work using electricity.

energy power to make something work. You need energy to get up and walk or run around.

filament thin piece of wire that gets hot and lights up inside a light bulb

infrared light that we cannot see with our eyes. Infrared light is used in television remote controls.

LED type of light that glows when electricity goes through it

material something that objects are made from.

muscles parts of the body that help us to move around

optical fibre thin thread that light signals are sent along

prism triangle shaped piece of glass that can be used to show all the colours of the rainbow

rainbow when all the colours in light are split up so you can see them

react do or change something. If you react to light, the light is a signal that makes you do something.

reflection when light bounces off a surface

surface top, or outside part of an object

ultraviolet light that we cannot see. Ultraviolet light comes from the Sun and can give us sunburn.

Index